BLACK MARKETS
WHITE BOYFRIENDS
and other acts of elision

BLACK MARKETS
WHITE BOYFRIENDS
and other acts of elision

by
Ian Iqbal Rashid

TSAR
Toronto
1991

The Publishers acknowledge generous assistance from
the Ontario Arts Council and the Canada Council.

Copyright © 1991 by Ian Iqbal Rashid
Except for purposes of review, no part
of this publication may be reproduced, in any form,
without prior permission of the publishers.

ISBN 0-920661-18-1

TSAR Publications
P.O. Box 6996, Station A
Toronto, Ontario, Canada
M5W 1X7

Front cover photo by Sunil Gupta from the exhibition Pretended Family Relationships
Author photo by Yasmin Karim
Cover design by Holly Fisher

With thanks and love
to
Albert Chevalier
and to
John Greyson

Acknowledgements

Some of these poems have been accepted for publication–some in a slightly different form–by *The Alchemist, Bazaar* (United Kingdom), *Canadian Literary Quarterly, Celebrasian, Cross World, Elixir, Khayal, Poetry Canada Review, Rites,* and *Toronto South Asain Review.*

The author would like to thank the Ontario Arts Council, the City of Toronto through the Toronto Arts Council, and the Toronto Lesbian and Gay Community Appeal for their financial support.

Contents

Introduction by Himani Bannerji *ix*

BLACK MARKETS

An/other Country 3
Redefinition 5
Re-Presentation 6
Black Market 7
Black Market 2: A May-December Romance 8
The Perils of Pedagogy 9
Fabled Territories 11
Bewitched, Bothered and Bewildered 13

THERE IS THIS TRICK...

There is this trick... 17
Now 20
There is this trick (2)... 21
Child 22
Schism: There is this trick... 23
Hot Property 25
New Moon 27
Over There 28

ENCHANTED EVENINGS

Hospital Visit 31
Hospital Visit (2) 32
Enchanted Evenings (or the Mourning After) 33
Could Have Danced All Night 36
Raw, flawed and asking more than we could bear... 38
Civilities 41
A Pass to India 43

By Way of an Introduction:
A Letter From Himani Bannerji

Dear Ian,

Sitting in Calcutta, reading your poetry which I brought with me from Canada, I am worried about form. Not yours, but mine. How to do the introduction to the first book of a friend's poetry, where the author/poet, not the friend, is what should matter to the world at large? I want to write about you, the friend/author, and me, the friend/reader, about both of us–reading/writing, constructing a poem for each of us, with a written page between us. Proof that though language/words speak us, we speak them as well. That is why so many poets and poems–so many readers and writers, and language, a river–double back on themselves. So I speak to your words and poems.

Who hears or over-hears?

I will write, I think, I will write you a letter.

Ian, our history as humans, and the history of art, is about separation, necessary and unnecessary, and about coming together, making–us or it–occasional, unbidden. The child must emerge from the womb, not only for a biological survival, but to be child, know mother; people pull up their roots from the earth only to marvel at trees, and lovers, necessarily broken into two from a con-joint body, if Plato is to be trusted, to search each other, for each other. Your poetry speaks to me about this being two–about two bodies, two minds, two beings in the world, which is essential if one must not live in a solitary confinement, or a hall of mirrors. And yet, as your pages tell, this two-ness and their coming together is not free of pain, nor of course without pleasure.

We exit through our orifices, or of the mother's, into the world, into the other and our own otherness, gasping for breath, grasping, as you have written, "an/other." And that holds for one and all. It is, and is not, simple, easy but necessary, indeed inevitable, in fact irresistible. Just life. And again, it is at the point of this realization that your poems add to my thoughts about "being," of involving another in the process, and the good and bad violence of our histories and relations. And, as I read your poems to him, on this still afternoon when life has reached the tips of our fingers, a man, a poet to be precise, suffering from an unease about life ending, the so-called Gulf War, says: "The answer is in the body. Why did it take so long to realize this?" This question (if it is that) does not require an answer really, but more a telling from other grounds, such as your poems, where body and mind, and other polarities, tear apart and come together, where love's pain and tenderness take hold of even a body where death to quote Garcia Federico Lorca, "has already laid its eggs in the wound."

And thus, what of violence? Or love's or death's openings and closures? Of that film in black and white which frames and scripts our brown, white lives? Who reads whose mind with the dark lamp of ambivalence, of desire and revulsion, pulsations of sex and pain? Does Hari Kumar create the Constable of the Raj even as he is unmade by him as one of your poems might suggest? How much do you create the white male lover of your dualist duels who holds you, puzzled, in thrall? Are such things permissible even to talk about? Are they "politically correct"–these continuous yet retractable surrenders to our opposites, the negative/positive vibrations of the cop and the man cruising in the blind alley, and the long, discerning, holding out resistance to degradation, the strip-search loss of dignity.

It seems you speak of much that is not "correct," not comfortable to linear psyches, and often unutterable–moving in the minefields, as you have written, with keys in hand like weapons. And of course, there is always that watching self-consciousness, sometimes resignation, which in your parchment nights of hospitals, looks like patience, and always in the end surprised by the body, your own or the other's. Finally, also always, a visitor from another planet—our India—re-collected in tourism, with its calligraphy all over your body, and its impersonal presence of a collective unconscious, that is both you and not you.

These are strong poems, Ian, and fine ones. They are the beginning of a kind of terrorism of imagination that might shock the thought police, in and around us, take an iron-file to what Blake once called the "mind-forged manacles" of both the so-called left (of whatever colour or sexual orientation) and the right. Of course you will need/need-to-go further, but this distance is already there—in the in-step of your poetry.

Much love,

Himani,
Calcutta
April 1991

BLACK MARKETS

An/other Country

All this new love of my parents' country:
We have bought the videotapes together,
bought the magazines and books,
all the advertisements,
each others' responses.
We watch the slides of your visit.
Your handsome face tanned, surrounded by mango trees,
planted above the poverty,
the moist beauty,
(which you think of blowing up and then framing,
building into your walls)
majesty imposed upon majesty.

Now I watch you watch Sergeant Merrick watch poor Hari Kumar.
And follow as the white man's desire is twisted,
manipulated into a brutal beating.
You are affected by the actor's brown sweating
body supple under punishment. What moves you?
The pain within the geometry of the body bent?
The dignity willed in the motions of refusal?
A private fantasy promised, exploding
within every bead of sweat?
Or is it the knowledge of later:
how my body will become supple
for you, will curve and bow to your wishes
as yours can never quite bend to mine.
What moves you then?

My beauty is branded into the colour of my skin,
my strands of hair thick as snakes,
damp with the lushness of all the tropics,
My humble penis cheated by the imperial wealth of yours.
Hari's corporal punishment, mine corporeal:
Yet this is also part of my desire.

3

Even stroking myself against your absence
I must close my eyes and think of England.

A Redefinition

I lie here on this vast rumpled ocean, your bed,
completely naked but for my skin
which is also a sheath.
This sheath itself you can make a weapon, and a fine one:
It gleams nut-brown or bronze or cocoa
or other such magazine words
polished by the sucking of maggots and pests,
waxed, with a veneer of spice and feces,
washed by urine which men have spurted against
make-shift dwellings by which I have lain.
I am a catastrophic beauty (this will make you smile)
–an insistence of immortality.
Through my pores are amplified the shouts
of street merchants and photogenic urchins,
(this makes your smile disappear, yes?),
the offensive cries of burning brides,
hopeless milk screaming inside their searing, succulent,
honey-coloured breasts. Listen carefully: hear
the music, melting, bubbling beyond...
so sweet, so sweet...

I am not even a complication, not worthy
of being one. My words enter the clarity
of your gaze like a blade but what comes back
is corn-flower blue, dazed, a trifle
embarrassed, no hurtful words, no afternoon
television dramatics...you reach for me, large
white spider against my darkness and I am
yours, now and for the first time.
For you see, my big, blonde, perfume-soaked Sahib,
you have, through your polite–your civilized–grace,
brought down my New World.

Re-Presentation

It seems the dead won't wake anymore
having drowned again in their histories and politics,
leaving me to wonder what is left of them
to disturb us, to climb in between.
All that is apparent is this telephone
and a slim chord of smoke
exhaled, a pile of clothes
sitting before me that I have worn
before you, changed and changed
again, it's a wonder that you kept track.
The numbers too have changed
and changed again, filed over and over
in books and in memory,
until one was filed for the last time,
like a weapon put away
useless because it had become eroded
or perhaps just absorbed by/
with the other strangers who have taken me in.

I trust kindness less than anger
but your voice comes through the phone
like music remembered which slips behind one
pushing all behind, until I
can't remember that particularly foul equation
of cologne and your sweat.

Black Market

Now you tell me that you can't hear the whispering,
that the tree bending under wind is not
a crooked-boned old man; the thin sliver of moon
you proclaim a slice of lemon pie,
I can't buy that.
I can see only a naked light against a dark low ceiling.
I'm a shadow paling away
in your golden-sunlight-against-sandstone glow.
Only if you choose to be, you say, sick-sweetly.

There's a colour picture
of you I saw just yesterday.
You sit, lean
-ing back in your chair, in no danger
of falling. Arms outstretched
luxuriously, you smile with charm, without
strain, about to speak: something
wondrous no doubt...a coloured balloon,
like in the comics. You look so capable,
so capable of such lovely things.

So...what to do?
Our worlds are available to us
at such unlike costs,
paid for so differently.
And this particular exchange of currency doesn't work.

Black Market: A May-December Romance

On our left, sir, we are passing a nearby island.
Now if you look carefully into the shadows
beyond the rockery and lush vegetation
you will realize that this is no cross standing
but a dark young man with aching open arms:
he is called strange siren
and we are told that he is cursed:
the song he sings so unfamiliar
that he himself is stranded.

Now listen, sir, and listen hard.
Listen beyond the motor rumblings of this meagre voyage.
Brace yourself, there's a deal to be made,
it will be difficult to get beyond
the harshness of the lyrics, the alien smell,
the colours too vibrant,
everything encrusted with difference,
the adjustments will be difficult to make.
But this island property is being offered
at a price that is a steal and your money
just isn't good elsewhere anymore.
It'll be taken here.

The Perils of Pedagogy

You hug your knees on top of the desk
and talk of dead Europeans in such a way
then make acrobatic leaps across continents
that leave me breathless and angry
yet I am surprised to find
myself touched by knobby knees
poking through fading
linen, your eyes are shiny, lit,
you speak wondrous images:
rum coloured warrior, the newness
of an island after a storm,
blood-tipped sword, bell clanging
in the night, a floating meaningful
handkerchief and the anguished disbelief
of a lovely, lost lady.

They are all yours for these moments,
in an alien heat, your singing
cigarette-sanded voice surrounds them—
and suddenly–you exhale
and it's all complete and punctuated,
a book of pictures coloured,
the last page turning to close...

And I am yours too,
(despite the hand up in the air
waving like a placard all semester,
despite my crumpling the feathers of Frye)
but not in strange Cyprus,
am here with you, wondering: your eyes,
your knees, how to possess such a glow?
"O! what hardness to dissemble."
How to tell you I don't
want any of this, I

want you. How to know
do I want this,
do I want you.

Fabled Territories

for Sunil Gupta

I

Where I am when he looks at me?
    Uncertain
if what he sees
is as fable territoried
as what I have myself
claimed a place where planted
upside-down in an earth so red-red rich
–Rajasthani red?–so
I(t) can't quite be believed

and sometimes fear(ed)

II

Where I am when you look at me
is the certainty of complete
worlds pictures-perfect, not jewel-like,
but messy–shoved in my mail box

and the relief of music
-scapes that can't be danced to
familiarity of a language
that modulates
my life maps
gravity, knowing, location,
the familiarity of a language I can not speak

III

Where I look when I look at me
is down and what I see
are feet marching through
a muddy uncertainty
no chart for this journey
no Berlitz phrases
just a sliding, spongy
familiarity in comfort
warm between my toes
again-familiar
again I am in shit.

Bewitched, Bothered and Bewildered

You will know of sorcery
when you taste the wine that I place before you,
read the cabala in how supple I bend,
see an odd flash of vermilion in the pencilled eye,
the roundness of a newly fed brown belly.
If you try to pry yourself loose
you will let in time and place and blood
to flow between us.
An opening will appear, others waiting to enter;
defeating your escape. I will become pliant
and submissive, I know my role.
You will want to stay.

I will allow you again, come in, come
inside, further and further
until you are in,
in me tasting
the spice on my skin feeling
the sweat in my hair moving
the earth under my nails remembering
the details from the Spartacus travel guide
which led you through the inexpensive twilights
which annexed themselves to the dawns that became
the one hundred and one nights that were your Subcontinent.

If you were to nail my footprint to the ground I would limp
and you might know a different future,
not this ciphering of limbs entwined,
tongues circling.
But you know not of such things.
You have shifted
and blood and time and place circulate
around and between us

–they are mine.
Together we will have you.
As you will have it.

THERE IS THIS TRICK...

There is this trick...

1.

There is this trick I knew
we met only on rain
-filled nights
all night

the wind would
carry
all by
the window
lashing

its history
against the pane
how my words used to slip
into the clear
lake of him

with ease
like a plunging dagger
with the ease of a Crusade

2.

My vague flirtations
were precious

pearls
that his cowboy-round
eyes would lasso along
with my history faraway
places roped in

by the rain
but now the meaning of you
to me is centrifugal
a force which has tossed
me here left

me blistering
on your bed
while you are on the other side
in mine
the space between us
an eye

3.

resilient calm
which stays
which defies all
lacerations...I wish now
for my rain

man sweet cherry
boy
the faint
down above
his lips a coolness
I long

to
taste to feel again
like wise
old solidity
no more the dusty dice

4.

Look
here is the rain
which gives the wind
a second
voice caustic

until it's subdued
and wet comes
down dark as I

would have you/him to me
speaking against all
your whispers
illness' lashing
fury subdued

as I come
down
moist
and
dark.

Now

Now, as I push it all gently
behind me, carefully applying my oar,
finding earth now, I hear hands
on word machine creating worlds,
full of easy rememberings, and futures intact,
from across the hall, as I wake,
staircase between us descending.

It is with me now, to be carried
onto the bank, wet sand to grass wet,
my knowing limited: the swift pianissimo of fingers
across the hairs of my belly, tenderness
rushing through an arc of curl on forehead,
the memory of dreams,
                        these piles of wonder.
In the doorway/emerging from the thicket
are suspended the new faces you show me, destined
for others, not for the man whose moments you filled,
then emptied, whose moments are filled
tracking, then tracing the in-step of your words.

There is this trick...(2)

There is this trick you do,
clever and quick.
I am walking with you, your flowers woven in my hair
and I am, like always, hopefully pulling at your sleeve,
waiting to be taken somewhere I haven't been.
And suddenly, yes, we are transported
and I am with you and my self,
both of you staring at me,
the features that I fear most,
that I fear I am, distorted.
And you handsome conjurer revealing both hands free,
holding them out for me even,
innocent and amazed, smiling;
No incantations, smiles,
saying that this is how it is,
how it ought to be,
The way that it is in this fun-house hall of horrors.
And it is. And I am.

Child

The most that you'll ever know
is that this place is a strange island:
this moment you climb into
an effortless achievement; lap,
kingdom, make-shift womb:
all which your clear eyes can trace.

We are on the floor
both of us cross-legged,
you sitting within me
meditating, miniature Buddha, contained,
surrounded by grotesque shadow.
Studying my blue chin,
contemplating the complexity of
paisley, playing in the curly black forest
beyond my shirt. Soon, restless, you'll crawl away,
no more spongy round eyes,
no more tiny little starfish of a hand
pulling at my big, big nose.

Schism: There is this trick...

My friend, a very young child
has found that a language surrounds her.
It is one that perhaps will not serve her needs
but at least it does not petrify her
as she looks at it
nor, I am convinced, will it become
petrified, museum around her.
Already she has inflected
it with a music that is all her own
and of many other places.
She may one day pound against or stroke its walls
but she will probably live her life within it.
I see how her everything shifts all the time
but for the moment there is a crowded chamber that she has
yet to locate, this place of "I" and "you,"
(you're cold, she says, hugging herself)
no sign yet of a passageway that
will inevitably lead her to that insistence
that every one of her experiences
belongs only to herself.

These quotients interest me
to the point of distraction.
I begin to wonder what it means when we are told,
those of us who will never be allowed to claim
this language as one of our own,
told by some that have discovered new worlds
where people have always lived that there is this trick,
something that *you* must do/read/say
to restart your heart.
That *you* have carried an alien burden
across an alien landscape.

That occasionally *you* must push; pull
up a clump of something fresh;
you must stomp and shout.
(And as everything shifts)
Told that you must be angry.

Hot Property

On the phone with you
trying heroically to save myself and failing
and I hear a click–yet another call waiting.
Inspiration–I decide to pretend
I'm drowning, my dark body
just barely visible in steam rising through a break,
flailing about below a frozen body of water,
helpless, unaccustomed to the cold,
coming from a tropical climate and all.
Save me. You do the work.
But you are annoyed, won't play
you see a different kind of transparency,
no ice, no danger of freezing.

Click quickly to the next caller
and become a mouth piece,
confident oracle if I am believed,
and I am, all the wisdom of the East
messenger, who has never been east of Montreal,
messenger who has not yet been revealed.
Even when I'm mute, it seems,
this one gathers my saliva in buckets
as it drips from my parted lips
and strains for discovery.

I click back
and you're still there
watching me now as I tread water.
The climate's become milder and I'm willing to swim.
You're willing to pull me onto terra firma.
A fair ground.
But in the same moment:
I catch my dark self swimming gracefully

in the mirror frame. Tropical fish.
I see a hook.
New trick.
It's simpler to stay put and wait.
Haul the fisherman in.

New Moon

My stomach rejects the night,
tosses it upward like a moon
until it rests in my mouth
lightly on my tongue.
I am mute. (My choice.)
If I could speak (your choice)
I would re-create you...

This is how it would work:
I would damn you for your beauty,
circumscribe a halo of cruelty
about your head.
Tell you that your failures
have gripped me like fingers
yet I have kissed them gently.

I am weary
of this, of
trying to make recreations
from failure.
There is no celestial body
on my tongue.
Just hundreds of miniscule
little balls, spiky, resilient
that have formed a film.
The silence:
our wise gifts to one another.

Over There

I patter across the floor, now
approaching stealth,
and you are there,
just like it says on the map, ready
with your weapon,
this space that I must pass through,
eyes closed, wishing that I could eliminate scent,
to be elsewhere, with the others who come
and go can leave
our bunker (who don't know about dancing
among land mines, keys and wallet in hand
like grenades) leaving for breath,
for warmth and touch, to survive,
leaving me here to blind you with rice
and too-hot curried concoctions;
camouflage, all the strategic gifts, this choreography
of give and take (which you chart as a rape),
words, which you decode
until these too are revealed
like the stain of pink that spreads
along the nape of your neck
and here, beached in the cold, memory
of the landscapes that emerge
on the twin islands
of your nipples,
highly detailed topography–
which I wish
I could not feel
passing against my tongue.

ENCHANTED EVENINGS.

Hospital Visit

In the Maze below
the echoes of cliches spill over
the deserted street:
Gestapo sirens splitting the ringing
of the bouncing sexual cash registers,
packaged so tight like so many little moans.
There is a heady smell left down there:
fear and sin and gasoline,
and the blood in the mouth taste of war.

And I sit while this thing
has got me by the hair–
with you beside me
as naked as a chicken's foot.
I must prepare.
(Herr Doktor, Herr Lucifer
is here: every touch a bribe, every
word so expensive.)

I place you in your white quiver
and draw you against me.
I wonder at the gravity of my predicament
and look down at my useless palms:
saturated rags. And you are burning up,
your body as dry as anger.
I cover you with my hands,
I will become your sweat.
And it's just as well that I re-arrange this analogy,
if just until the morning.
For even without assistance, a July morning can kill.

Hospital Visit (2)

I remember a sense
was made: those previous, writhing
crucifixions; tenderness behind hangmen's eyes,
tacit smiles,
sweaty voyagers
traversing a sticky Styx,
discovering an occasional irony:
one of us to be
(for a few hours anyway)
the man that our state truly desires.

Then later:
we would breakfast.
Straight-backed
as the yellow clamour of morning danced
    delightedly
over our battle scars.
And redefined, we would love each other.

Now you are not the desired one.
We play out another kind of bondage: diaphanous,
venomous serpents chain your form
to an ice-box white.
The memory is mine to recognize.
Upright and brown, clammy and helpless,
I find a thin wisp of longing.
I push it forward.
It floats between us.

Enchanted Evenings (or the Mourning After)

I

After another hard memorial service, the eighth this year, Ian and the boys decide to dispense with the elegies, sit around with a few beers and watch old tapes of Dynasty...

    I leave you broken, shattered
    –untouchable like the jagged bits of a fluorescent bulb.
    This time there's nothing left in your bag of tricks.
    Mists can only be conjured up elsewhere,
    in distant incandescent mythologies.
    Your new world is just dark.

II

Alexis stops driving. Her white gloved hand turns off the ignitions. She slowly begins to turn her head to see who's been following.

(Collective gasp).

"Fabulous"

"It's just like Orpheus."

    But driving away in my car
    I decide to stop,
    decide to turn back for you,
    but not out of kindness...
    There is something stuck in my head,
    not quite formed yet.
    You will mold it to completion.

    I will observe what it is to be human,
    to be a broken thing.

III

A few beers later and several fast-forwarded episodes later we're finally willing to get a bit maudlin. We've now put some Warhol-Edie Sedgewick thing on the VCR....

    You used to sing to the drunks on the subway.
    Startling creation:
    pigeon-chested madonna
    Tossing white shock,
    kicking gleaming vogue legs
    and laughing, always laughing.
    Spilling laughter on the amazed masses down below.

    Now, waiting for another train,
    your smile makes me sad;
    a thin deceit, badly disguised
    that I must make myself believe in.
    Necessary knife (as I smile back)
    plunging into my own deaf flesh.

IV

"He loved that Edie Sedgewick biography that George Plimpton didn't edit. Boy he loved that book."

"He sure knew how to perpetuate a stereotype..."

"Quiet, here comes that dance scene..."

    Oh, but I wanted to stay with that galvanized queen
    who draped dead animals around herself
    and danced to an unyielding beat,
    who lived in a night-scented story.

What happened?
Why the disappearing act in your eyes every
time I look? What is that beaten thing
watching from behind the cage of your skull?

V

"Remember that Halloween Party when he came as Libby Holman..."

"He thought nobody would know who Libby Holman was."

"Everybody knows who Libby Holman was."

You try and purr like a tigress. I smile
(Or more accurately: he accomplishes, assembles a smile.)
Your failure, you call it, is awkward for me.
I don't know how to pity you, don't want to know.
Will away battered eyes and anguished wringing of hands.
We'll pretend nothing has changed, we'll feed off memory.
Voices combined, we'll absorb the whispering
of the knowing train, we'll overpower the thin dry scream
of a star plummeting to earth.

Could Have Danced All Night

I

I once used to dream of being held knowingly by a man
on whom I would not look.

Then this all came again, the embrace held
in the ease of a dance, held within your hands small
yet capable and roped with thick vein.
And when I tried, it didn't surprise me
to be able to look into your eyes like mine,
the rough colour of night, into your shy, pie face.

Standing together tonight I long for the anise
taste of Thai basil on your skin,
your ass and thighs resplendent
in strobes of evening's light.
Tonight I would dance with you across an alien landscape.
We could fly. ("I'm positive.")
But this night finds our legs rooted, knotted,
planted painfully like a flag. ("I've tested positive.")

II

Tonight, I watch you walking away,
wheeling your burden before you into the night.
Fists jab my thighs on either side.
Fists which mean to unclench hold
fingers which mean to interlock
with yours, like pieces of a puzzle
join into a picture of two men dancing.

Tonight movement is limited:
from hand to mouth to mind.

Tobacco, caustic laughter in the lungs,
the careful sipping of our herbal teas,
the careful sipping of our everything-will-be-all-rights.

Raw, flawed and asking more than we could bear...[*]

I

Walking through the trees like fingers searching
a filing cabinet.
Time is opening up the sky.
No more the dark animal hide of night.
Morning nudges, urges speed and efficiency.
Soon a shoeless new day.
The blood still rushes through me,
a thousand constant ants.

I meet a necessary angel behind a rustling of leaves.
I notice how he carries his history with him
has placed it carefully under his tongue.
His stories are told to me,
I am bathed in them,
a liquid which can ease all injury.
But the eyes of wounds are left behind
to search over him,
prying, looking for too-familiar truths, infection.

II

I find his late mouth
and contain it so now there is only
one storyteller
the story mine to tell.

I pioneer into a perilous history as a champion must
without protection, unsafe-d, plunging forward,
revelling at the prospect of eluding a deadly foe.
(The narrator laughs, shocked
at our hero's audacity

just as the hero himself laughs at peril:
no formulas in rebellion,
only guilt in the face of deaths.

This is a marginal story,
a poem about margins of safety,
the difference between costs.
And of course, there are no lines
to follow in the margins of a page,
no guidance, no history,
except for the faint arcs of ink
where writer and hero meet
in mortal embrace.)

My story ends with the night
but I take it with me
a house in which I live
like Aesop who found his way
and his place in darkness.

III

His starry glow is thrown
on me, bent metallic smile,
curses like splashes of liquid bright,
(like the sanctioned pleasures of fireworks)
a crisp flag of lust which the surprise,
the breadth of denial can snap
to attention,
like the end of a fantasy
like the surprise of newness that a beginning can offer
fingers like a cage, a wild-haired platinum
that rises through the cap,
I hear the kicking against a belly even as heat
pounding against my darkness
feel it through and through layers of skin and cloth ...

The light comes on again

and I am still here, coiled, panting,
shoeless on this slab of stone,
bloodied as if ripped from a birth.

*From a poem by Adrienne Rich

Civilities

I

He is charmed by
the muscles used
in the faces that I make,
these gentle veneers of affluence
which I wear, like the wings of flies,
no buzz, all flutter
which I will toward him
outward:
hot empty air
which perhaps carries dust,
the dead cells of others.
Funny how some people can survive
feeding only on movement.

Elsewhere, now.
Dead-end alley, dark, closed, like a purple cauldron.
We brew a meagre, libidinous soup,
our testicles echoing against each other
and suddenly we are not alone.
There is such a large, noisy glare...

II

Policeman on me
policeman on him
policeman says pervert

and he, pants down
nods yes, why not, somebody has to be,
so you can be policeman

policman on me says paki

bare hand on billy stick,
gloved hand pulling at my cock.

I look at him, surprised.
Nothing does me in more than
this particular kind of wisdom
behind soulless blue eyes.

A Pass to India

I take it with me
along with my bundle of belongings
that soon will seem to float beside me constantly,
an absence of metaphor
which my parents live with/out,
no dreams of snow,
home is a place without light
the dark continent
prize won for a victor for whom they mediated
a prize which mediates my narrative,
this place of my birth which
after it was conquered conquered
so they had to leave as I leave now
carrying the papers of a man whom I imagine
might vanish, becoming a man like the men
I've never known, disappeared;
trying to finish a story
suggested by a gaze at history,
a story told by old photographs
and older women trying
to redress the damage of absence
and early acts of elision,
a story whose open end holds me often
like a fist–snake tight–
God(dess)-like, serpent embrace,
except to caress me now and again, now,
mocking my obsession,
this open hand of a story with
its teasing mishaped fingertip of a subcontinent.

And I leave
reading one of two epic poems,
which governs a struggle that will not vanish

in a plane that zips open the sky like a myth
exposing its soft little-boy's belly,
leaving stiff vestments behind; leaving an anger behind
with the buildings that we are tunnelling by with a roar,
leaving for a place as impenetrable as a cell
under attack from a virus.